And the Winner Is ...

Amazing Animal Athletes

Written by **Etta Kaner**

Illustrated by **David Anderson**

Kids Can Press

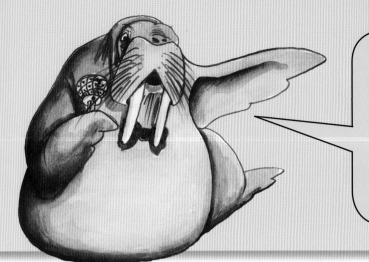

Welcome to the World Animal Games — that's WAG for short. Top athletes from habitats around the world will be competing for the gold! Exciting, isn't it, Cockatoo?

Habitats

Coastline — land that borders the sea

Desert — dry land with few plants and little rainfall

Grassland — a large area of land covered with grasses

Forest — a dense growth of trees, bushes and plants covering a large area

Mountain — peaked land higher than a hill

Ocean — a large body of salt water

Savanna — grassland with some trees

Tropical rain forest — warm, dense evergreen forest with heavy rainfall

Tundra — treeless frozen land with mosses, lichens and small shrubs

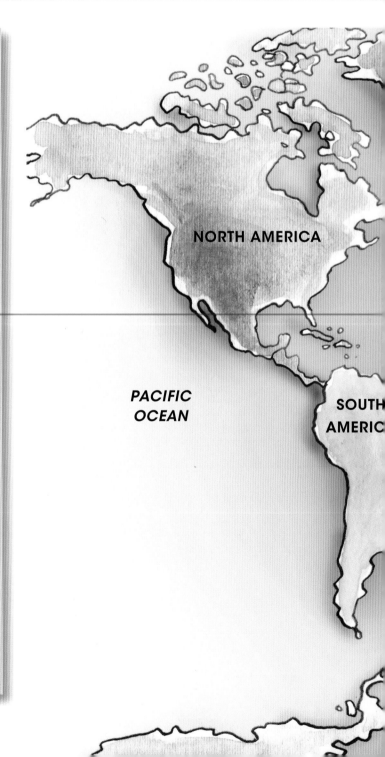

NORTH AMERICA

PACIFIC OCEAN

SOUTH AMERICA

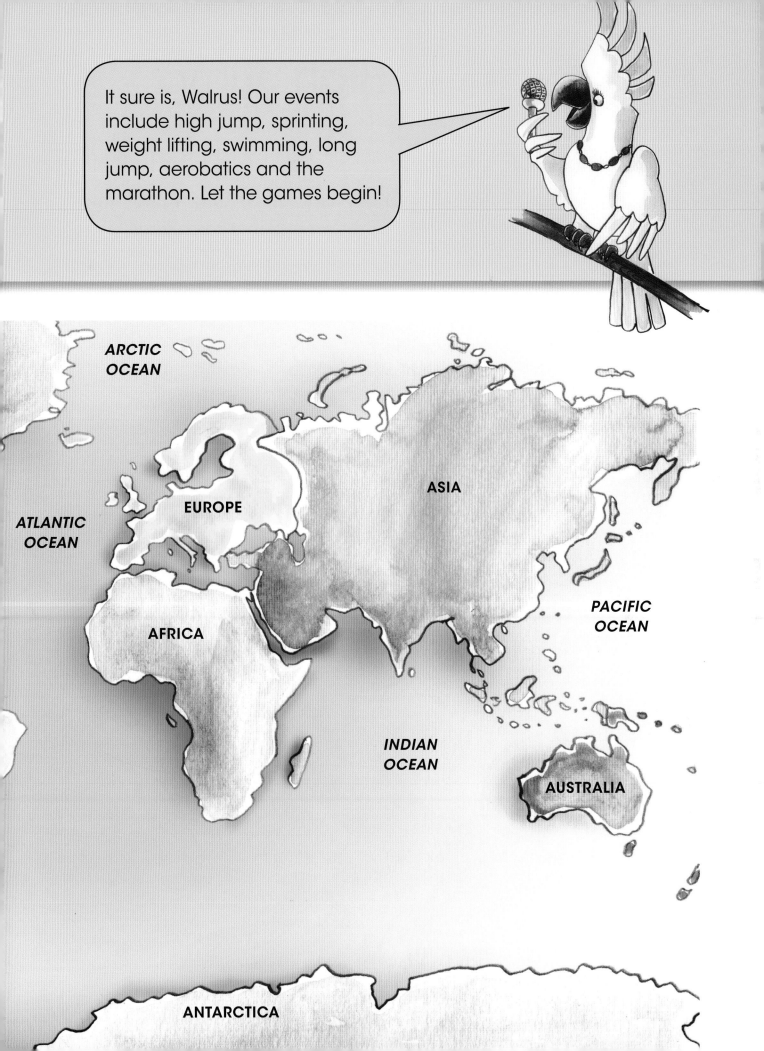

High Jump

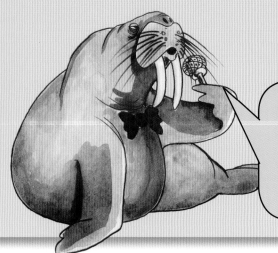

We're right on time for the high-jump event. The athletes will be judged on how many times their own height they can jump. That's fair since they are such different sizes.

Flea
Class: insect
Home: worldwide
Habitat: other animals
Food: blood

Puma
Class: mammal
Home: North, Central and South America
Habitat: mountains, savannas, forests, deserts
Food: small animals

High Jump 10 a.m.

Sorry, I didn't see you.

Hey, watch it!

It looks like they're ready to start. And there goes Puma. Wow, what a jump! The crowd goes wild. Or I should say *wilder*! Can anyone beat that?

Hip, hip, hooray!

And the winner is …

Klipspringer
Class: mammal
Home: Africa
Habitat: rocky hills in savannas
Food: plants

Red kangaroo
Class: mammal
Home: Australia
Habitat: savannas and open forests
Food: plants

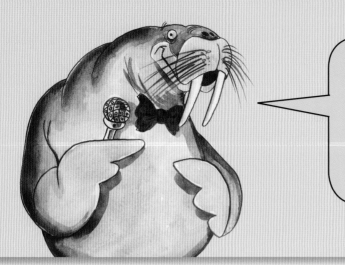

What a surprise! Who would have thought that this tiny insect, the size of ... well, the size of a flea, could jump 150 times its own height?

There are over 2000 kinds of fleas in the world.

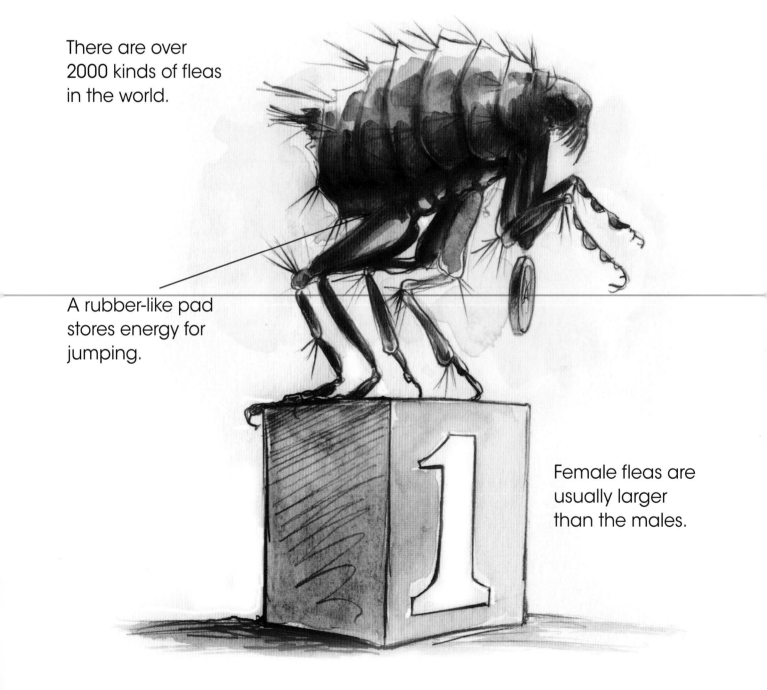

A rubber-like pad stores energy for jumping.

Female fleas are usually larger than the males.

This must be a dog flea. They jump higher than cat fleas. I bet dog fleas are smarter, too. Who would want to live on a cat? Let's see how high humans can jump.

The human high-jump record is 2.45 m (96.46 in.). That's less than two times the jumper's height. Not very much when compared to a flea. I bet that really bugs human high jumpers.

How high can you jump?

Sprinting

And they're off and running. Look at them go! Ostrich and Quarter Horse are neck and neck. But Brown Hare is bounding along with Cheetah right on her tail.

Brown hare
Class: mammal
Home: worldwide
Habitat: worldwide except polar regions
Food: plants

American quarter horse
Class: mammal
Home: worldwide except polar regions
Habitat: all except oceans and tundra
Food: grass, hay

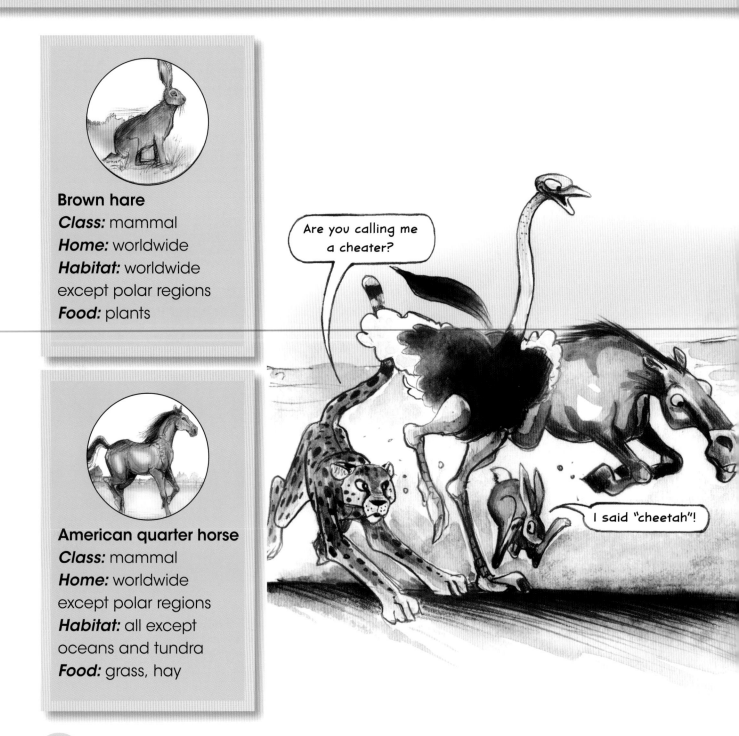

Amazing speed for such a little one!
But Cheetah will not be outdone.
He's cutting in and gaining speed.
Can he win the race again this year?

I'm hoarse from yelling.

Whoo's in the lead?

And the winner is …

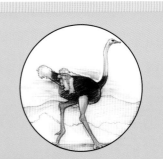

Ostrich
Class: bird
Home: Africa
Habitat: savannas, deserts
Food: plants, insects, small animals

Cheetah
Class: mammal
Home: Africa
Habitat: savannas
Food: small and medium-sized animals

Well, Cheetah has done it again. This is the fourth time he has won the gold in sprinting. Today, he reached a speed of 112 km/h (70 m.p.h.).

Large nostrils inhale extra air while running.

One stride can be as long as four bathtubs laid end to end.

Sharp claws grip the ground to help the cheetah push forward.

Earlier, I asked Cheetah how he does it. He said it's all in the way his body is built. His long legs and flexible spine help him take looong strides. Are humans as quick on their feet?

The human record for running the 100-meter dash is 9.58 seconds. The fastest time for a cheetah over the same distance is 5.95 seconds. It looks like animals win — paws down.

How fast can you run?

Weight Lifting

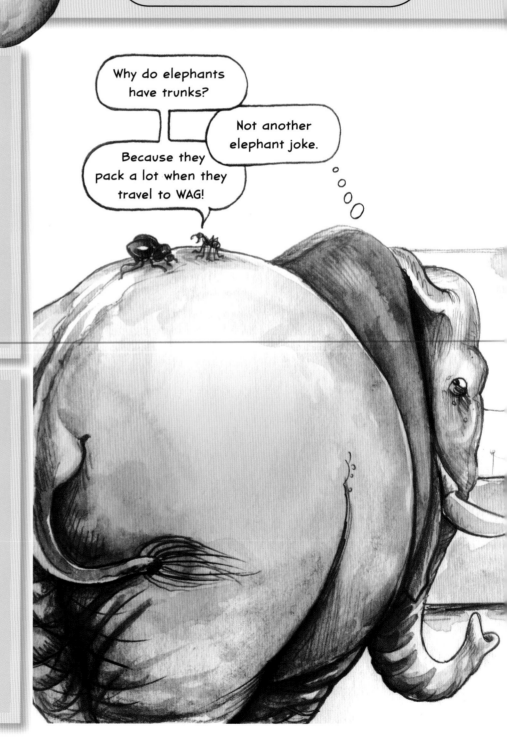

It's so quiet in the stadium you can hear a pin drop. The crowd is holding its breath to see how much Gorilla will lift.

Why do elephants have trunks?

Not another elephant joke.

Because they pack a lot when they travel to WAG!

African bush elephant
Class: mammal
Home: Africa
Habitat: savannas, open forests
Food: plants, fruit

Rhinoceros beetle
Class: insect
Home: worldwide except polar regions
Habitat: tropical rain forests
Food: rotting plants and fruit

So far, Leafcutter Ant has lifted 10 times her body weight. I can't see Gorilla beating that. He's such a show-off. He's always throwing his weight around!

This was billed as a big event!

And the winner is …

Leafcutter ant
Class: insect
Home: Central and South America
Habitat: tropical rain forests
Food: fungus

Gorilla
Class: mammal
Home: Africa
Habitat: tropical rain forests, mountain forests
Food: plants, fruit

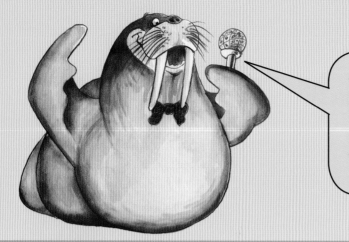

Wow! Who would believe it? Rhinoceros Beetle supported an object 100 times her own weight! How is that possible?

The male rhinoceros beetle has horns but the female doesn't.

Some rhinoceros beetles can be as big as your hand.

Females have very strong leg and body muscles.

Her training includes digging through rotten wood and soil to lay eggs in a deep hole. She also pushes through forest litter looking for food. I wonder how humans stack up.

A human weightlifting champ was able to lift 394 kg (868.6 lbs.). That's a lot, but it's only 4.6 times his body weight. He might want to take lessons from that six-legged wonder, the rhinoceros beetle.

How much can you lift?

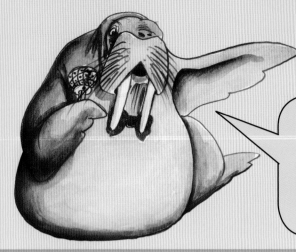

Swimming

And they're off! But wait! This is supposed to be a swimming event. Sailfish, Gentoo Penguin and Sea Lion are all leaping through the air. Is that against the rules?

Gentoo penguin
Class: bird
Home: Antarctica
Habitat: rocky coastlines
Food: small fish, krill, squid

Orca
Class: mammal
Home: worldwide
Habitat: oceans
Food: large fish, marine mammals

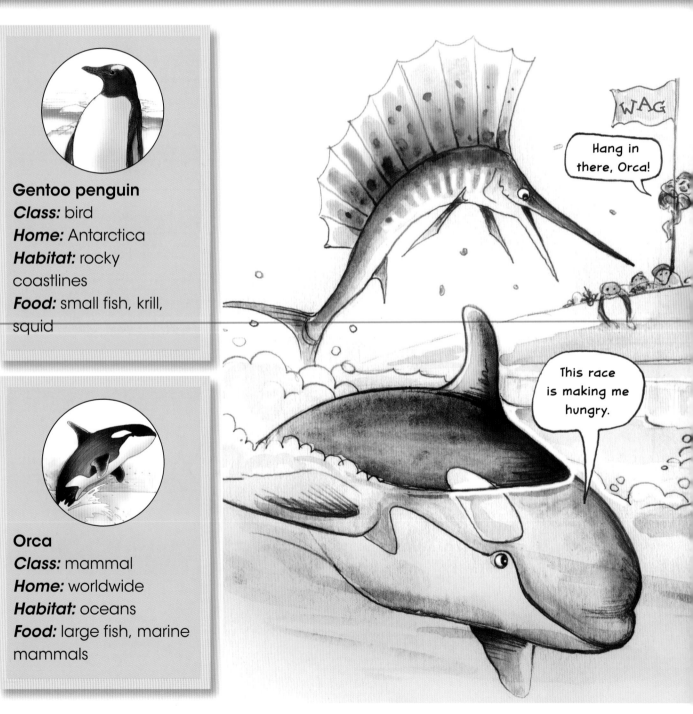

Nope. It's called porpoising. It uses less energy than swimming straight through water. Orca is the only one shooting through the water. Will it hurt his game?

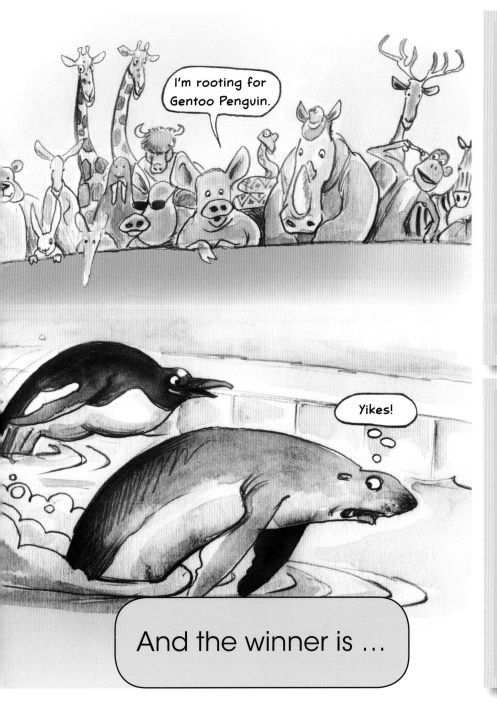

I'm rooting for Gentoo Penguin.

Yikes!

And the winner is …

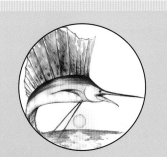

Sailfish
Class: fish
Home: Atlantic and Pacific Oceans
Habitat: warm parts of oceans
Food: small fish, squid, octopus

Sea lion
Class: mammal
Home: Pacific Ocean
Habitat: oceans and rocky coastlines
Food: fish, crabs, squid

What a performance! Sailfish swam at a speed of 109 km/h (67.7 m.p.h.). That's faster than a car driving on the highway. And did you see those colorful stripes on her body?

The sailfish's large fin, or sail, can instantly open up like a fan.

Sailfish use their bills to hit and stun their prey.

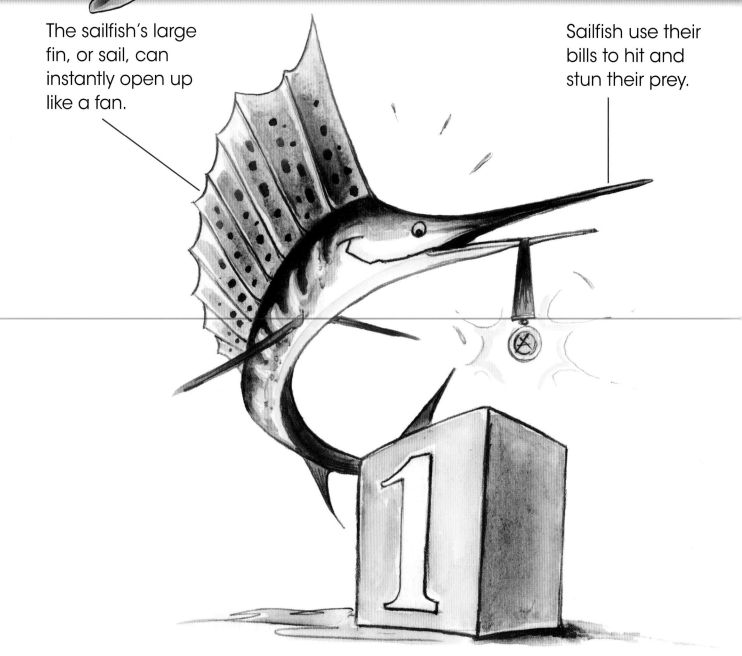

While hunting, it uses the sail to herd schools of fish.

Weren't they amazing? Sailfish usually flash those colors when they're excited about hunting. I guess she was eager to win this race. I bet human swimmers don't even come close to this speed.

No contest here! The world record for a human swimmer is 7 km/h (4.35 m.p.h.). That's the speed of a brisk walk. All of our animal athletes swam faster than that.

How fast can you swim?

Long Jump

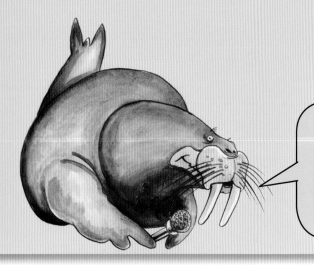

The crowd is in an uproar! The judges are hopping mad at Grasshopper! And no wonder. He flew during his jump. He should be disqualified. Hmmph!

Grasshopper
Class: insect
Home: worldwide except polar regions
Habitat: all except oceans and tundra
Food: plants

Kangaroo rat
Class: mammal
Home: North America
Habitat: deserts
Food: seeds

With Grasshopper out of the way, Jumping Spider and Rocket Frog might have a chance to win. But it won't be easy. Kangaroo Rat has already jumped 45 times his body length!

You've got to be kidding!

Foul play!

And the winner is …

Jumping spider
Class: arachnid
Home: worldwide except polar regions
Habitat: all except oceans and tundra
Food: small insects

Striped rocket frog
Class: amphibian
Home: Australia
Habitat: forests
Food: insects, worms, spiders

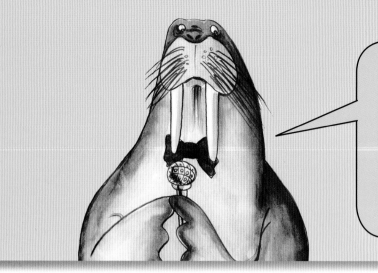

That was some jump! I've never seen anything like it. Striped Rocket Frog jumped 55 times his own body length. That's like a human jumping the length of a football field!

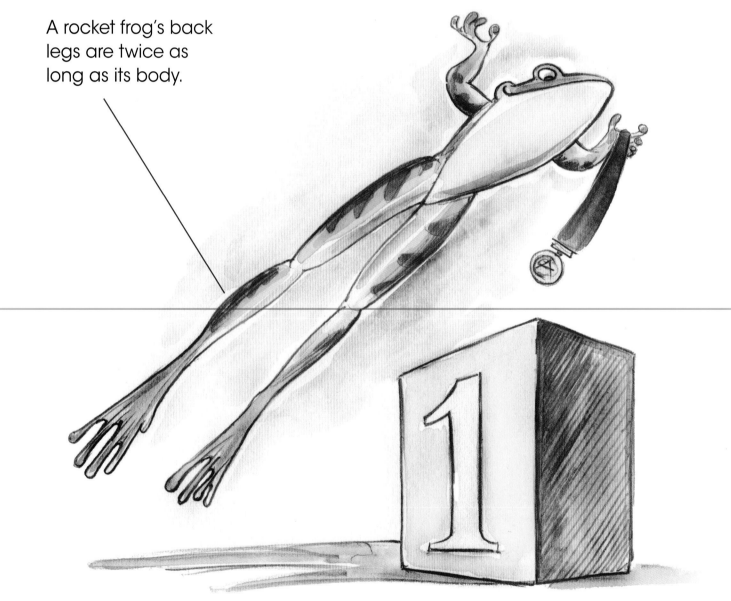

A rocket frog's back legs are twice as long as its body.

It's a type of tree frog but it can't climb trees.

Its narrow body helps it move easily through air and water.

Just look at those powerful back legs. Those muscles make up one-third of Rocket Frog's body weight. No wonder he moves like a rocket. Let's check out the human long jumpers.

The human world record for long jump is 8.95 m (29.4 ft.) That's less than five times the height of the athlete's body. Our animal athletes are ahead by leaps and bounds.

How far can you jump?

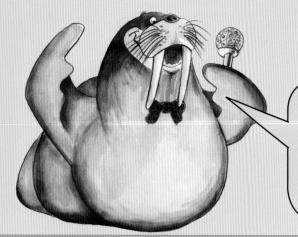

Aerobatics

It looks like our athletes are still warming up. There goes Flying Dragon Lizard. Nice glide! And Orangutan is giving his powerful arms a good workout.

African crowned eagle
Class: bird
Home: Africa
Habitat: forests and tropical rain forests
Food: small mammals

Orangutan
Class: mammal
Home: Asia
Habitat: tropical rain forests
Food: fruit, leaves, insects

Flying Snake has some pretty smooth moves. But look at Crowned Eagle. Those roller-coaster swoops will be hard to beat. I'm betting on the bird for this one!

Flying isn't only for the birds.

You call that flying?

And the winner is …

Flying dragon lizard
Class: reptile
Home: Asia
Habitat: tropical rain forests
Food: small insects

Flying snake
Class: reptile
Home: Asia
Habitat: tropical rain forests
Food: lizards, frogs, birds, bats

There's no doubt about it. Flying Snake is the judges' favorite. They loved the way she whipped her body through the air but never lost control. I wonder how she does it.

The flying snake glides in an S-shape.

It spends most of its time in trees.

It glides to catch prey and avoid predators.

She flattens her body and shapes it like an airplane wing. As she glides, air rushing underneath her body gives her lift. No way humans can compete with that!

The human aerial skiing champ did a record two triple-twisting triple somersaults in the air. To get height and speed, she first skied down a ramp at 72.4 km/hr (45 m.p.h.). Flying snakes just drop off a high branch to do their aerobatics.

Marathon

Yawn. It's been three days since our marathon athletes started. They're covering incredible distances. Gray Whale is churning through the water toward California. Monarch Butterfly is flapping her way to Mexico.

Bar-tailed godwit
Class: bird
Home: Alaska, New Zealand
Habitat: tundra, coastlines
Food: crustaceans, insects

Monarch butterfly
Class: insect
Home: North and Central America
Habitat: grasslands
Food: nectar

Our two bird athletes are flying even farther. It looks like our judges are going to be waiting a very long time until the athletes complete this last event.

Get a moo-ve on!

I just might have time to finish this sweater.

And I thought I was slow.

Wake me up when it's over.

And the winner is ...

Pacific golden plover
Class: bird
Home: countries on Pacific Ocean
Habitat: coastlines
Food: crustaceans, insects, berries

Gray whale
Class: mammal
Home: Pacific Ocean
Habitat: ocean, coastlines
Food: crustaceans

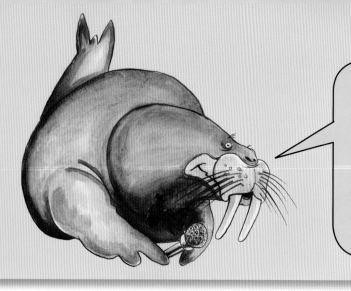

This is unbelievable! Bar-tailed Godwit flew 11 500 km (7146 mi.) in just eight days. She flew nonstop from Alaska to New Zealand without eating or drinking. She must have trained super hard for this event.

While migrating, parts of the bar-tailed godwit's brain sleeps.

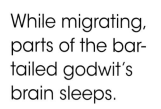

Wind passes smoothly over its sleek feathers while flying.

During migration, its muscles are bigger to support its heavier body.

You're right. Before the race, she ate extra food to double her weight in fat. Burning fat gave her energy during her flight. You've got to hand it to those birds. We, I mean *they*, never give up. Can humans match this?

The champion human ultramarathon runner ran 1000 km (621.4 mi.) in 5 days. At that speed, he would need almost two months to run the same distance as the bar-tailed godwit flew.

ALASKA

NEW ZEALAND

How far can you run before you need to stop?

Thanks for stopping by. We've enjoyed being your hosts.

See you at next year's World Animal Games!

For Yael and Ora — amazing winners both! — E.K.

Deep appreciation for the help of entomologists Donna Stockton and Karin Moll. Also, my heartfelt thanks to editors Karen Li and Stacey Roderick, who are always creative, thoughtful, patient and inspiring; to Julia Naimska for her clever design; and to David Anderson whose wonderful illustrations make me laugh!

Kids Can Press acknowledges the financial support of the Government of Ontario, through the Ontario Media Development Corporation's Ontario Book Initiative; the Ontario Arts Council; the Canada Council for the Arts; and the Government of Canada, through the CBF, for our publishing activity.

Published in Canada by
Kids Can Press Ltd.
25 Dockside Drive
Toronto, ON M5A 0B5

Published in the U.S. by
Kids Can Press Ltd.
2250 Military Road
Tonawanda, NY 14150

www.kidscanpress.com

Edited by Karen Li and Stacey Roderick
Designed by Julia Naimska

This book is smyth sewn casebound.
Manufactured in Shenzhen, China, in 10/2012 through Asia Pacific Offset

CM 13 0 9 8 7 6 5 4 3 2 1

Library and Archives Canada Cataloguing in Publication

Kaner, Etta
And the winner is — : amazing animal athletes / written by Etta Kaner ; illustrated by David Anderson.

ISBN 978-1-55453-904-8

1. Animal locomotion — Juvenile literature. 2. Animal mechanics — Juvenile literature. I. Anderson, David, 1952 June 7– II. Title.

QP303.K35 2012   j591   C2012-904398-2

Kids Can Press is a **corus**™ Entertainment company